TEXAS

TEXAS
Valerie Bodden

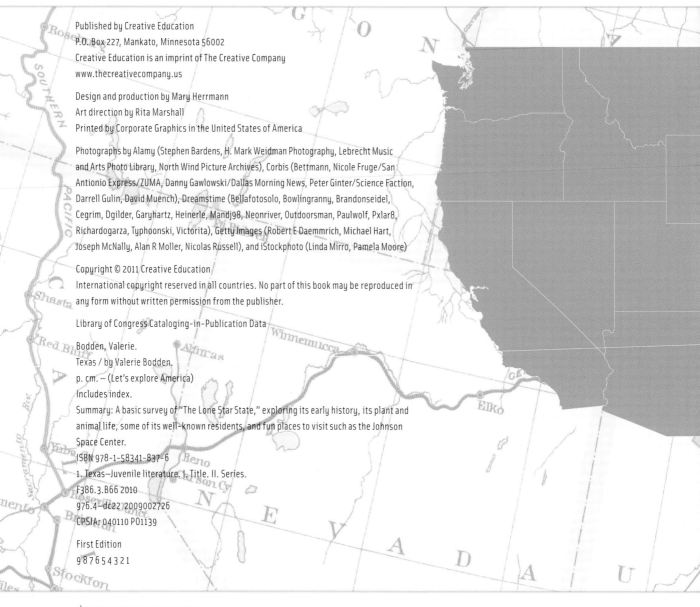

Published by Creative Education
P.O. Box 227, Mankato, Minnesota 56002
Creative Education is an imprint of The Creative Company
www.thecreativecompany.us

Design and production by Mary Herrmann
Art direction by Rita Marshall
Printed by Corporate Graphics in the United States of America

Photographs by Alamy (Stephen Bardens, H. Mark Weidman Photography, Lebrecht Music
and Arts Photo Library, North Wind Picture Archives), Corbis (Bettmann, Nicole Fruge/San
Antionio Express/ZUMA, Danny Gawlowski/Dallas Morning News, Peter Ginter/Science Faction,
Darrell Gulin, David Muench), Dreamstime (Bellafotosolo, Bowlingranny, Brandonseidel,
Cegrim, Dgilder, Garyhartz, Heinerle, Mandj98, Neonriver, Outdoorsman, Paulwolf, Pxlar8,
Richardogarza, Typhoonski, Victorita), Getty Images (Robert E Daemmrich, Michael Hart,
Joseph McNally, Alan R Moller, Nicolas Russell), and iStockphoto (Linda Mirro, Pamela Moore)

Library of Congress Cataloging-in-Publication Data

Bodden, Valerie.
Texas / by Valerie Bodden.
p. cm. – (Let's explore America)
Includes index.
Summary: A basic survey of "The Lone Star State," exploring its early history, its plant and
animal life, some of its well-known residents, and fun places to visit such as the Johnson
Space Center.
ISBN 978-1-58341-837-6
1. Texas—Juvenile literature. I. Title. II. Series.
F386.3.B66 2010
976.4—dc22 2009002726
CPSIA: 040110 PO1139

First Edition
9 8 7 6 5 4 3 2 1

C CREATIVE EDUCATION

Texas is a state in the southern part of America. It is a big state. Texas became a state in 1845. Texas is nicknamed "The Lone Star State." This is because its flag has one star on it.

TOP, THEN LEFT TO RIGHT:
- The Alamo (a building that was a church and then a fort) in San Antonio, Texas
- An old map of Texas
- A statue of a Texas Ranger (a kind of cowboy policeman)
- Texas cowboys driving cattle in the 1800s
- A cowboy on his horse

The Caddo **American Indians** were some of the first people to live in Texas. They were there before it was a state. Alonso Álvarez de Piñeda (*uh-LOHN-soh AHL-vuh-rayz day pee-NYAY-duh*) was one of the first non-Indians to explore Texas. More people moved to Texas after that.

TOP, THEN LEFT TO RIGHT:
• *An American Indian in Texas*
• *American Indians making pots*
• *A famous battle at the Alamo between soldiers from Mexico and Texas*
• *An early Texas church built by people from Spain*
• *Texans posing for a picture in the late 1800s*

TOP, THEN LEFT TO RIGHT:
- *Huge rocks in the Grapevine Mountains*
- *A Texas lake*
- *A forest of pine trees in eastern Texas*
- *A beach in the city of Corpus Christi, Texas*

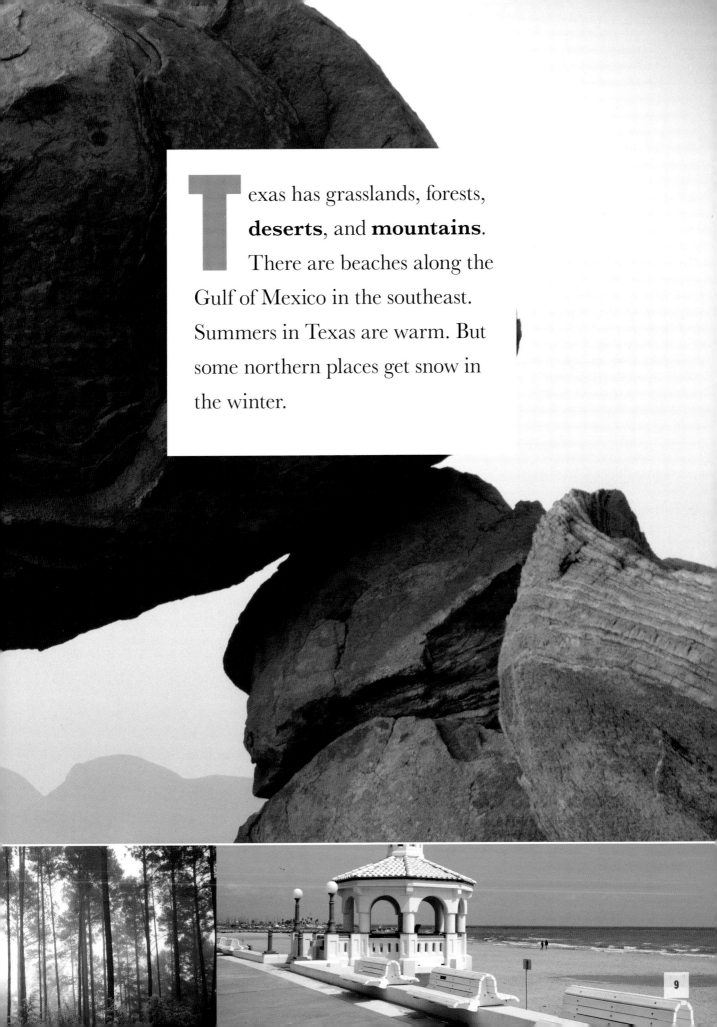

Texas has grasslands, forests, **deserts**, and **mountains**. There are beaches along the Gulf of Mexico in the southeast. Summers in Texas are warm. But some northern places get snow in the winter.

TOP, THEN LEFT TO RIGHT:

- A Texas farmer harvesting (collecting) cotton
- A pile of watermelons
- Texas rattlesnakes
- Cacti called prickly pear
- A mule deer

Farmers in Texas grow cotton and wheat. Lots of wildflowers grow in Texas. Pine trees grow in some areas. **Cacti** grow in the desert. Deer and rabbits live in Texas. So do snakes.

Texas's state flower is the bluebonnet. The bluebonnet is a blue and white flower. Texas's state bird is the mockingbird. The mockingbird is a small, white and gray bird. Texas's state tree is the pecan tree. The pecan tree produces tasty pecan nuts.

TOP, THEN LEFT TO RIGHT:
- *Bluebonnets growing along a Texas road*
- *A mockingbird*
- *Pecan nuts*
- *A close-up view of Texas bluebonnets*

Lots of people live in Texas. Some of them make airplanes. Some are construction workers. Others farm or drill for oil.

Lance Armstrong is a famous bicyclist from Texas. He won a race called the Tour de France seven times. Presidents Dwight D. Eisenhower and Lyndon B. Johnson were from Texas, too.

TOP, THEN LEFT TO RIGHT:
- *A cowboy roping a calf, or young cow*
- *President Dwight D. Eisenhower (at right)*
- *Bicyclist Lance Armstrong*
- *President Lyndon B. Johnson (at center)*
- *The Texas state flag*

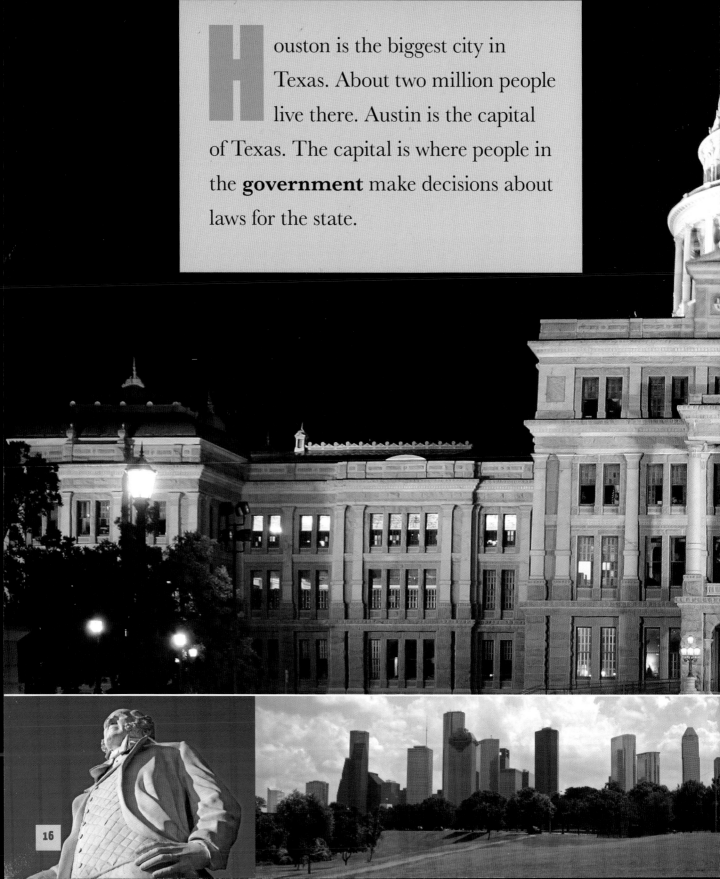

Houston is the biggest city in Texas. About two million people live there. Austin is the capital of Texas. The capital is where people in the **government** make decisions about laws for the state.

TOP, THEN LEFT TO RIGHT:

- *The state capitol (main government building) in Austin*
- *A statue of a Texas hero named Sam Houston*
- *Tall buildings called skyscrapers in Houston*
- *The inside of the state capitol*
- *A bridge in Austin*

17

Every year, lots of people visit Texas. Some learn about space shuttles at the Johnson Space Center. Others play on Texas's beaches. People can find big fun in the big state of Texas!

TOP, THEN LEFT TO RIGHT:
- *A young man playing on a Texas beach*
- *Fishing in a Texas river*
- *The field of the Dallas Cowboys football team*
- *Equipment at the Johnson Space Center*
- *People swimming in Galveston, Texas*

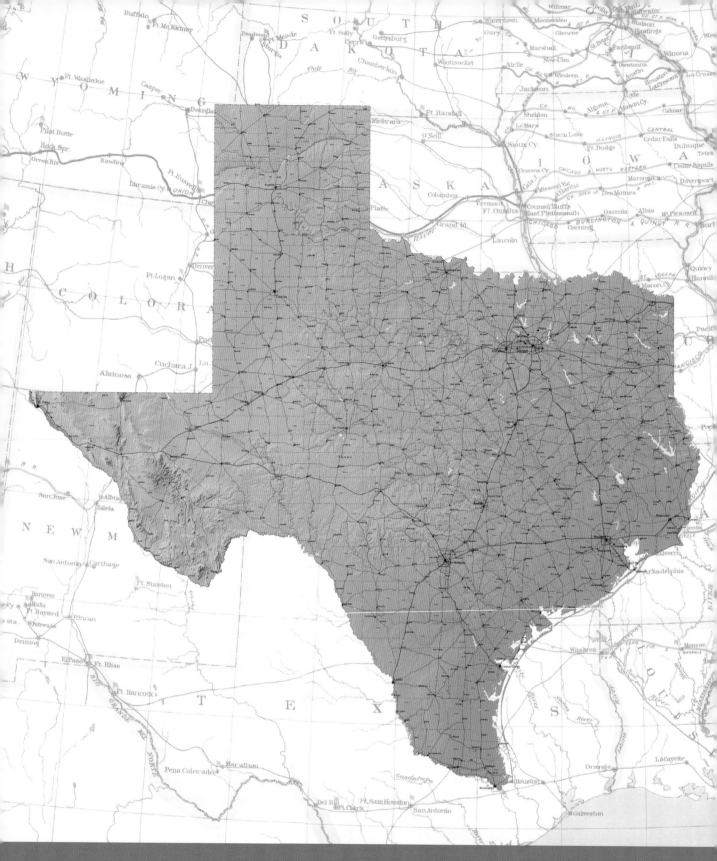

FACTS ABOUT TEXAS

First year as a state: *1845*

Population: *24,782,302*

Capital: *Austin*

Biggest city: *Houston*

Nickname: *The Lone Star State*

State bird: *mockingbird*

State flower: *bluebonnet*

State tree: *pecan tree*

An oil rig for drilling oil from under the ocean

GLOSSARY

American Indians—people who lived in America
before white people arrived

cacti—desert plants that have spines (sharp spikes)
instead of leaves; a single plant is called a cactus

deserts—big, hot areas sometimes covered with sand

government—a group that makes laws for the people
of a state or country

mountains—very tall, steep hills made out of rock

READ MORE

Bredeson, Carmen. *Texas*. New York: Children's Press, 2002.

Crane, Carol. *L Is for Lone Star: A Texas Alphabet*.
Chelsea, Mich.: Sleeping Bear Press, 2001.

LEARN MORE

Enchanted Learning: Texas
http://www.enchantedlearning.com/usa/states/texas/
index.shtml
This site has Texas facts, maps, and coloring pages.

Kids Konnect: Texas
http://www.kidskonnect.com/content/view/207/27
This site lists facts about Texas.

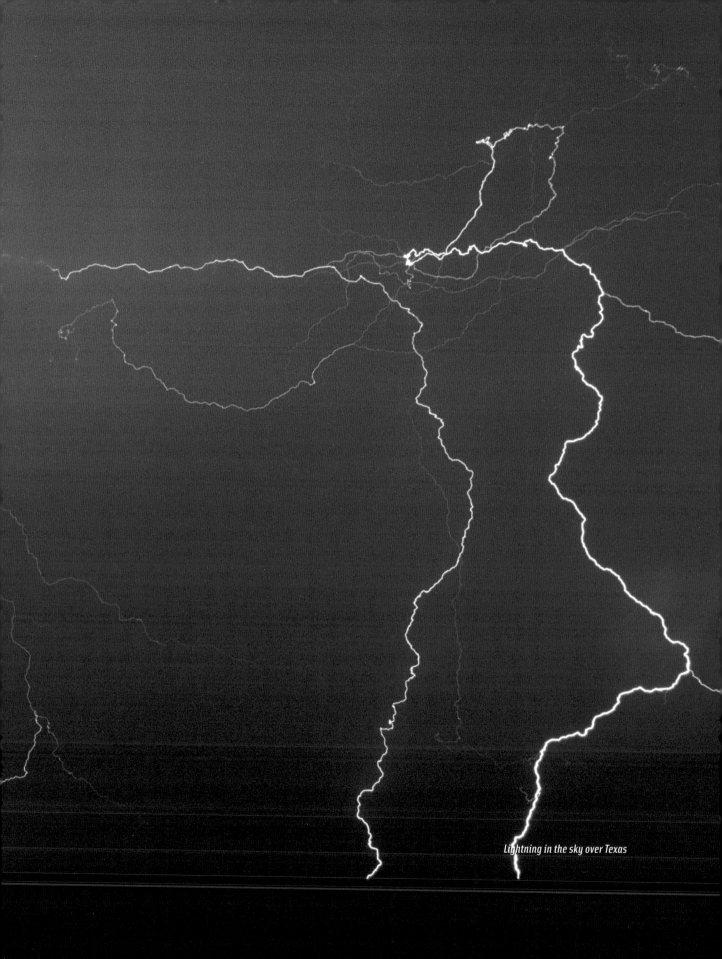

Lightning in the sky over Texas

A fisherman in the Gulf of Mexico near Texas